We Wish You a Merry Christmas

and other festive poems

Also by Chris Riddell and available from Macmillan

Poems to Fall in Love With

Poems to Live Your Life By

Poems to Save the World With

We Wish You a Merry Christmas

and other festive poems

CHOSEN AND ILLUSTRATED BY

Chris Riddell

MACMILLAN

For Ann

Published 2022 by Macmillan Children's Books
an imprint of Pan Macmillan
The Smithson, 6 Briset Street, London EC1M 5NR
EU representative: Macmillan Publishers Ireland Ltd, 1st Floor,
The Liffey Trust Centre, 117–126 Sheriff Street Upper
Dublin 1, D01 YC43
Associated companies throughout the world
www.panmacmillan.com

ISBN 978-1-5290-8642-3

Pan Macmillan does not have any control over, or any responsibility for,
any author or third-party websites referred to in or on this book.

1 3 5 7 9 8 6 4 2

A CIP catalogue record for this book is available from the British Library.

Printed and bound by CPI Group (UK) Ltd, Croydon CR0 4YY

Contents

from Now Thrice Welcome, Christmas

Now thrice welcome, Christmas,
  Which brings us good cheer,
Minced pies and plum porridge,
  Good ale and strong beer;
With pig, goose and capon,
  The best that may be,
So well doth the weather
  And our stomachs agree.

George Wither

We Wish You a Merry Christmas

We wish you a merry Christmas,
We wish you a merry Christmas,
We wish you a merry Christmas
And a happy New Year.

> *Good tidings we bring*
> *To you and your kin,*
> *We wish you a merry Christmas*
> *And a happy New Year.*

Now bring us some figgy pudding,
Now bring us some figgy pudding,
Now bring us some figgy pudding,
And bring some out here.

Chorus

For we all like figgy pudding,
For we all like figgy pudding,
For we all like figgy pudding,
So bring some out here.

Chorus

And we won't go until we've had some,
And we won't go until we've had some,
And we won't go until we've had some,
So bring some out here.

Chorus

Anon.

3

Jingle Bells

Dashing through the snow
In a one-horse open sleigh,
Over the fields we go,
Laughing all the way;
Bells on bob-tail ring,
Making spirits bright,
What fun it is to ride and sing
A sleighing song tonight!

Jingle bells, jingle bells,
Jingle all the way!
Oh what fun it is to ride
In a one-horse open sleigh!
Jingle bells, jingle bells,
Jingle all the way!
Oh what fun it is to ride
In a one-horse open sleigh!

James Pierpoint

The Christmas Life

*'If you don't have a real tree, you don't
bring the Christmas life into the house.'*
Josephine Mackinnon, aged 8

Bring in a tree, a young Norwegian spruce,
Bring hyacinths that rooted in the cold.
Bring winter jasmine as its buds unfold –
Bring the Christmas life into this house.

Bring red and green and gold, bring things that shine,
Bring candlesticks and music, food and wine.
Bring in your memories of Christmas past.
Bring in your tears for all that you have lost.

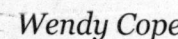

Bring in the shepherd boy, the ox and ass,
Bring in the stillness of an icy night,
Bring in a birth, of hope and love and light.
Bring the Christmas life into this house.

Wendy Cope

6

Christmas at Four Winds Farm

With the tambourine tinkle of ice on the moor
and the winter moon white as a bone,
my grandad and his father
set out to bring Christmas home.

A wild winter wizard had grizzled the gorse
and spangled the splinter-sharp leaves,
when the light of their wind-swinging lantern
found a magical Christmas tree.

From the glittering town at the end of the dale
the carols grew sweeter and bolder,
as my grandad's smiling father
carried Christmas home on his shoulder.

Maureen Haselhurst

Green Magi

Peace is the season's anthem
And goodwill the battle cry.

And on this holy of holly nights
pine needles on fire pierce the frost

the heavens give their best high fives
and snowmen packed tightly warm
follow the stars of children's hands

for snowmen are made out of love
and mean human kind no harm.

John Agard

Mistletoe

For over a thousand years, it has been traditional
to hang mistletoe indoors around Christmas time.

Bird's beak brings me to this branch.
Bird's beak bites down, bursts berry,
and seed-me burrows into bark.

Gulping its goodness, I grow –
a glowing globe. Tree goes garnet,
then grey. I go on, golden-green.

When the world is winter-white,
you want me in your warm home.
I ward off woe. I whisper, *welcome*.

Rachel Piercey

9

The Holly and the Ivy

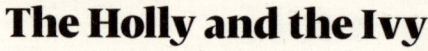

The holly and the ivy,
When they are both full grown,
Of all the trees that are in the wood,
The holly bears the crown.

The rising of the sun
And the running of the deer,
The playing of the merry organ,
Sweet singing in the choir.

The holly bears a blossom
As white as lily flower,
And Mary bore sweet Jesus Christ
To be our sweet Saviour.

The holly bears a berry
As red as any blood,
And Mary bore sweet Jesus Christ
For to do us sinners good.

The holly bears a prickle
As sharp as any thorn,
And Mary bore sweet Jesus Christ
On Christmas Day in the morn.

The holly bears a bark
As bitter as any gall,
And Mary bore sweet Jesus Christ
For to redeem us all.

The holly and the ivy,
When they are both full grown,
Of all the trees that are in the wood,
The holly bears the crown.

Anon.

Just Doing My Job

I'm one of Herod's Henchmen.
We don't have much to say,
We just charge through the audience
In a Henchman sort of way.
We all wear woolly helmets
To hide our hair and ears,
And wellingtons sprayed silver
To match our tinfoil spears.
Our swords are made of cardboard
So blood will not be spilled
If we trip and stab a parent
When the hall's completely filled.

We don't look VERY scary,
We're mostly small and shy,
And some of us wear glasses,
But we give the thing a try.
We whisper Henchman noises
While Herod hunts for strangers,
And then we all charge out again
Like nervous Power Rangers.
Yet when the play is over
And Miss is out of breath
We'll charge like Henchmen through the hall
And scare our mums to death.

Clare Bevan

Angels

We are made from light.
Called into being we burn
Brighter than the silver white
Of hot magnesium.
More sudden than yellow phosphorus.
We are the fire of heaven;
Blue flames and golden ether.

We are from stars.
Spinning beyond the farthest galaxy
In an instant gathered to this point
We shine, speak our messages and go,
Back to the brilliance.
We are not separate, not individual,
We are what we are made of. Only
Shaped sometimes into tall-winged warriors,
Our faces solemn as swords,
Our voices joy.

The skies are cold;
Suns do not warm us;
Fire does not burn itself.
Only once we touched you
And felt a human heat.
Once, in the brightness of the frost,
Above the hills, in glittering starlight,
Once, we sang.

Jan Dean

Street Lights

The town leapt a little, tonight,
As the Christmas lights came on.
Everyday streets became more important
And even the darkest pathways glistened.
Stars and snowflakes
Angels and reindeer
Flashed and flickered a holy-white whisper,
Making our town,
Our ordinary, brick and tarmac town,
Sparkle like a frosted castle
In a far-off, frozen land.

Coral Rumble

from A Child's Christmas in Wales

Looking through my bedroom window, out into the moonlight and the unending smoke-coloured snow, I could see the lights in the windows of all the other houses on our hill and hear the music rising from them up the long, steadily falling night. I turned the gas down, I got into bed. I said some words to the close and holy darkness, and then I slept.

Dylan Thomas

17

First Snow in the Street

I did not sleep last night.
The falling snow was beautiful and white.
I dressed, sneaked down the stairs
And opened wide the door.
I had not seen such snow before.

Our grubby little street had gone.
The world was brand-new, and everywhere
There was pureness in the air.
I felt such peace. Watching every flake
My heart felt more and more awake.

I thought I'd learned all there was to know
About the trillion million different kinds
Of swirling frosty falling flakes of snow.
But that was not so.
I did not know how vividly it lit
The world with such a peaceful glow.

Upstairs my parents slept,
Yet I could not drag myself away from that sight
To call them down and have them share
The mute miracle that was everywhere.
The snow seemed to fall for me alone.
How beautiful the grubby little street had grown!

Brian Patten

The Snowman

Mother, while you were at the shops
and I was snoozing in my chair
I heard a tap at the window
saw a snowman standing there

He looked so cold and miserable
I almost could have cried
so I put the kettle on
and invited him inside

I made him a cup of cocoa
to warm the cockles of his nose
then he snuggled in front of the fire
for a cosy little doze

He lay there warm and smiling
softly counting sheep
I eavesdropped for a little while
then I too fell asleep

Seems he woke and tiptoed out
exactly when I'm not too sure
it's a wonder you didn't see him
as you came in through the door

(oh, and by the way,
the kitten's made a puddle on the floor)

Roger McGough

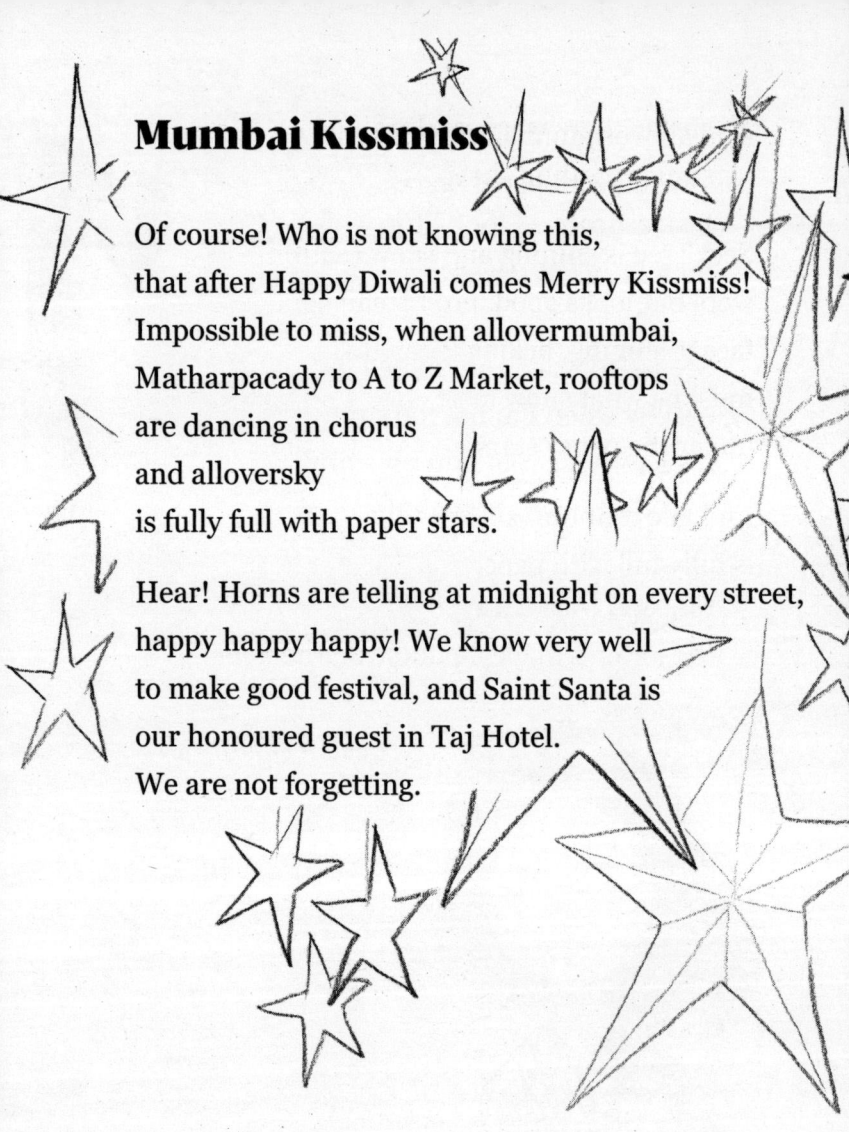

Mumbai Kissmiss

Of course! Who is not knowing this,
that after Happy Diwali comes Merry Kissmiss!
Impossible to miss, when allovermumbai,
Matharpacady to A to Z Market, rooftops
are dancing in chorus
and alloversky
is fully full with paper stars.

Hear! Horns are telling at midnight on every street,
happy happy happy! We know very well
to make good festival, and Saint Santa is
our honoured guest in Taj Hotel.
We are not forgetting.

And allovermumbai alloversky
is fully full with paper stars.

See! Tree is shining and snow (cotton-
wool but looks good, no?) Small child also
face is shining, licking icing, this
must be what snow tastes like
under the paper stars.

And allovermumbai alloversky
is fully full with paper stars.

Imtiaz Dharker

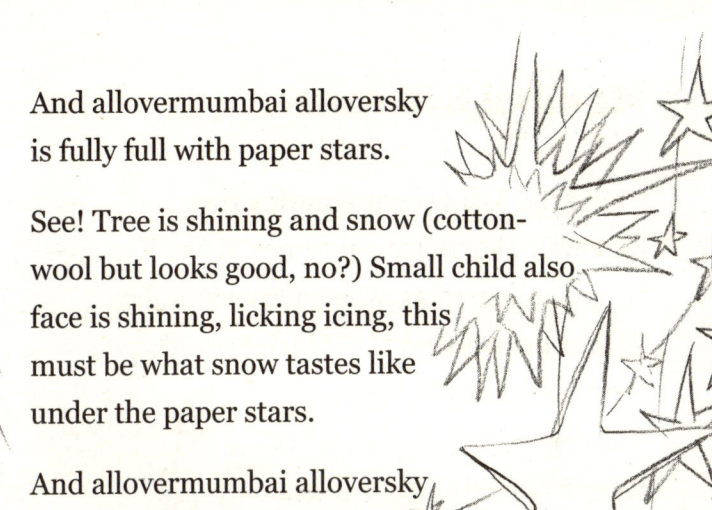

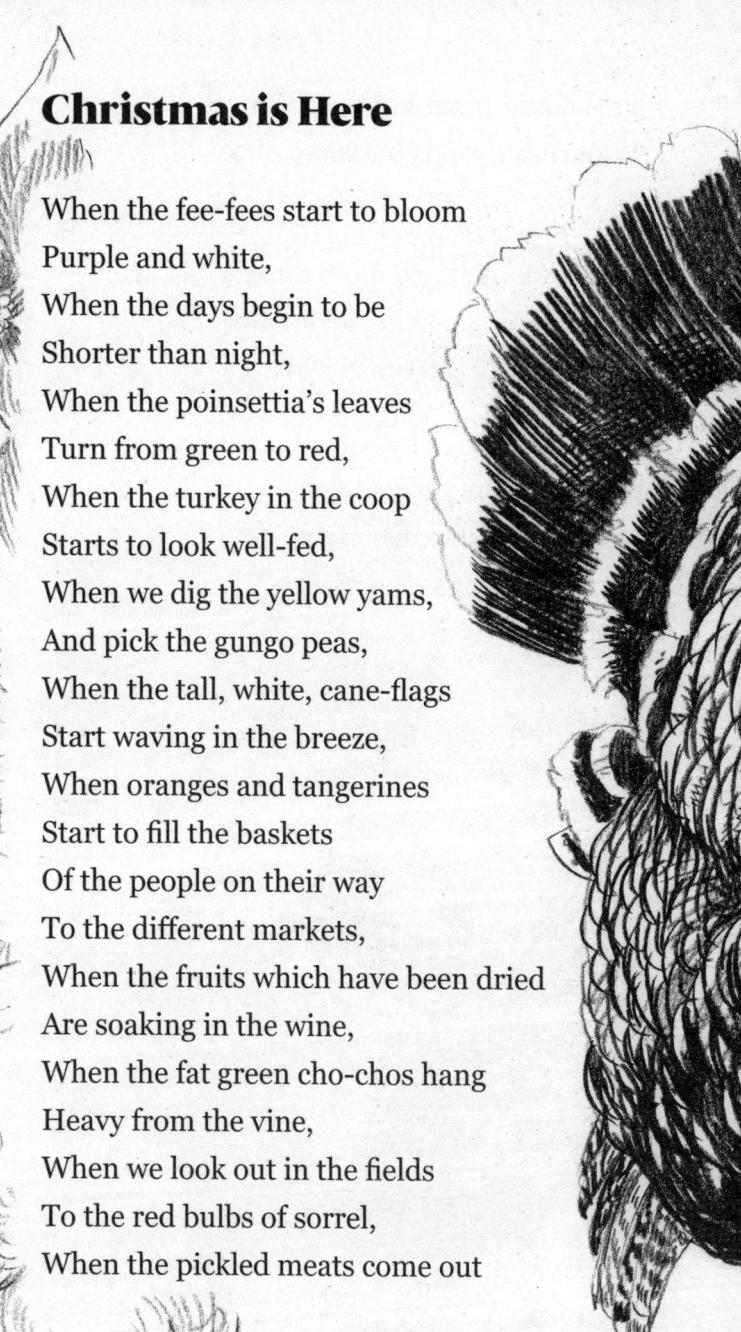

Christmas is Here

When the fee-fees start to bloom
Purple and white,
When the days begin to be
Shorter than night,
When the poinsettia's leaves
Turn from green to red,
When the turkey in the coop
Starts to look well-fed,
When we dig the yellow yams,
And pick the gungo peas,
When the tall, white, cane-flags
Start waving in the breeze,
When oranges and tangerines
Start to fill the baskets
Of the people on their way
To the different markets,
When the fruits which have been dried
Are soaking in the wine,
When the fat green cho-chos hang
Heavy from the vine,
When we look out in the fields
To the red bulbs of sorrel,
When the pickled meats come out

From their place in the brine barrel,
When each meal contains a slice
Of avocado pear,
Then we know for certain that
Christmas time is here.

Valerie Bloom

Skating at Night

(from *The Prelude*)

And in the frosty season, when the sun
Was set, and visible for many a mile
The cottage windows through the twilight blazed,
I heeded not the summons. Clear and loud
The village clock tolled six; I wheeled about,
Proud and exulting like an untired horse
That cares not for his home. All shod with steel,
We hissed along the polished ice in games
Confederate, imitative of the chase
And woodland pleasures – the resounding horn,
The pack loud bellowing, and the hunted hare.
So through the darkness and the cold we flew,
And not a voice was idle. With the din,
Meanwhile, the precipices rang aloud;
The leafless trees and every icy crag
Tinkled like iron; while the distant hills
Into the tumult send an alien sound
Of melancholy, not unnoticed, while the stars,
Eastward, were sparkling clear, and in the west
The orange sky of evening died away.

Not seldom from the uproar I retired
Into a silent bay, or sportively
Glanced sideway, leaving the tumultuous throng,
To cut across the image of a star
That gleamed upon the ice; and oftentimes,
When we had given our bodies to the wind,
And all the shadowy banks on either side
Came sweeping through the darkness, spinning still
The rapid line of motion, then at once
Have I, reclining back upon my heels,
Stopped short; yet still the solitary cliffs
Wheeled by me – even as if the earth had rolled
With visible motion her diurnal round!
Behind me did they stretch in solemn train,
Feebler and feebler, and I stood and watched
Till all was tranquil as a dreamless sleep.

William Wordsworth

Snow in the Suburbs

Every branch big with it,
Bent every twig with it;
Every fork like a white web-foot;
Every street and pavement mute:
Some flakes have lost their way, and grope back
    upward, when
Meeting those meandering down they turn and
    descend again.
The palings are glued together like a wall,
And there is no waft of wind with the fleecy fall.

28

A sparrow enters the tree,
　　Whereon immediately
A snow-lump thrice his own slight size
Descends on him and showers his head and eyes,
　　And overturns him,
　　And near inurns him,
And lights on a nether twig, when its brush
Starts off a volley of other lodging lumps with a rush.

　　The steps are a blanched slope,
　　Up which, with feeble hope,
A black cat comes, wide-eyed and thin;
　　And we take him in.

Thomas Hardy

Going Home

I remember going home,
every year, after I left home,
to the echo of that
childhood Christmas comfort.
To the lit Christmas tree
and the aroma of baking,
to the comfort blankets of
family and fireside
and that welcome release
of responsibilities.
I remember the silence
of the street on Christmas morning,
the day stuffed full with
expectations, everyone talking
excitedly, the dog
desperate for a walk.
I remember the boy I was,
the boy who couldn't wait to leave
that cold seaside town,
to escape, to some better place
elsewhere.

I remember it all, decades back,
swept away with the pine needles.
And yet, it's what I do,
It's what we all do, time-travelling
in the sweet December gloom,
all of us, forever, going home.

Brian Moses

Christmas Eve

On Christmas Eve
it is so late
that even Mum and Dad
are fast asleep in bed.

I stand at the top of the stairs

The house is warm
and the tree lights glow.

I can smell mince pies
and anticipation.

I make a wish.

Roger Stevens

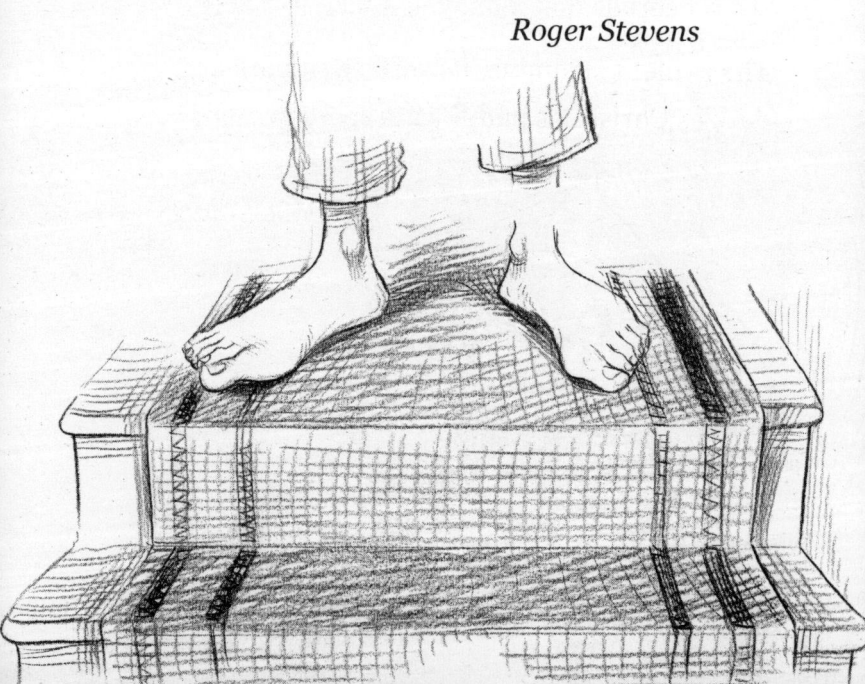

We Are Not Alone

Captain's Log. Starship Saturnalian.
Earth year 2030, day 358 –
The new drive worked! We've tracked the alien
spacecraft that vanished from earth's orbit late

last night. We followed its fantastic leap
across the galaxy and now can see
its sledge-like shape dropping in steep
descent to a planet. Incredibly

a single cosmonaut whose suit glows red
clings to its tail and holds long ropes to steer
a group of prancing creatures: from each head
sprout aerials that make them look like deer.

The planet's steaming, its surface smooth and
dark as Christmas pudding. Prepare to land!

Dave Calder

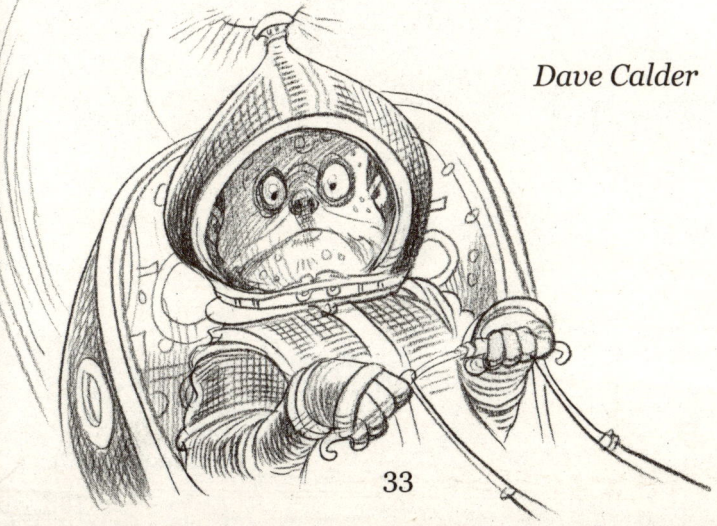

You Do Not Need a Chimney for Santa Claus to Come

You do not need a chimney
for Santa Claus to come
You do not need a fireplace
to hand your stocking from

That stuff is just from telly
Do not believe the films
You do not need a great big house
for Santa to come in.

He's got a sleigh, for goodness sake
and loads of elves at hand;
Mrs Claus behind the scenes
computing all the plans;

Flying, glowing reindeer
galloping the Christmas air
Of course he can manage
a few quick flights of stairs –

the top flat of a tower block;
the barge on a canal;
a spare room in a friend's house;
a hostel; a hotel

So snuggle into sleep now
and don't listen to anyone
who says you need a chimney
for Santa Claus to come

Hollie McNish

A Visit from St Nicholas

'Twas the night before Christmas, when all through the
   house
Not a creature was stirring, not even a mouse;
The stockings were hung by the chimney with care,
In hopes that St Nicholas soon would be there;
The children were nestled all snug in their beds,
While visions of sugar-plums danced in their heads;
And mamma in her 'kerchief, and I in my cap,
Had just settled our brains for a long winter's nap –

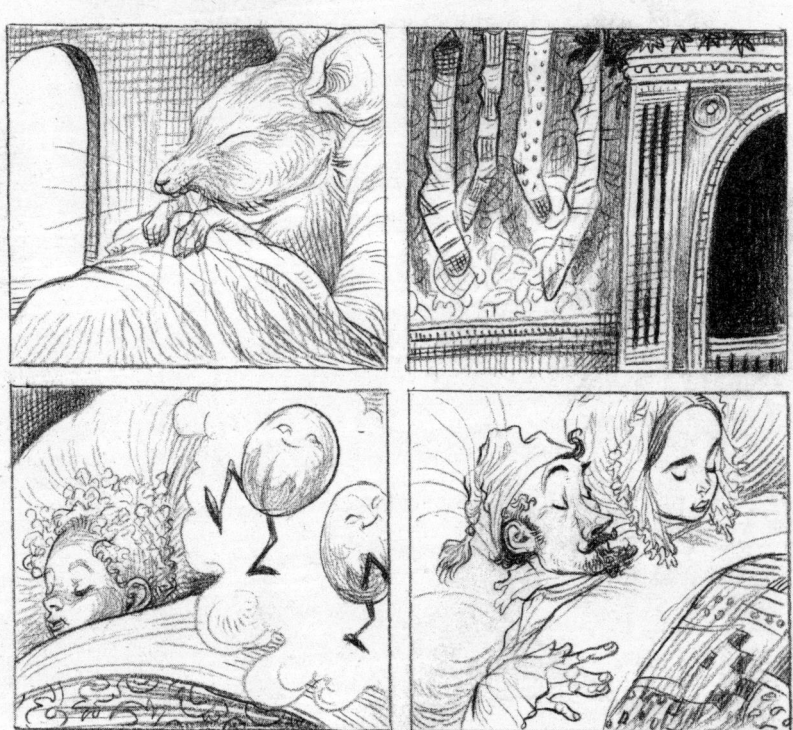

When out on the lawn there arose such a clatter,

I sprang from my bed to see what was the matter.

Away to the window I flew like a flash,

Tore open the shutters, and threw up the sash.

The moon, on the breast of the new-fallen snow,
Gave the lustre of midday to objects below;
When what to my wondering eyes should appear,
But a miniature sleigh and eight tiny reindeer,
With a little old driver, so lively and quick,
I knew in a moment it must be St Nick.

More rapid than eagles his coursers they came,
And he whistled, and shouted, and called them by name:
'Now, Dasher! now, Dancer! now, Prancer and Vixen!
On, Comet! on, Cupid! on, Donder and Blitzen!
To the top of the porch! to the top of the wall!
Now dash away! dash away! dash away all!'

As leaves that before the wild hurricane fly,
When they meet with an obstacle, mount to the sky;
So up to the house-top the coursers they flew
With the sleigh full of toys, and St Nicholas too.
And then, in a twinkling, I heard on the roof
The prancing and pawing of each little hoof.
As I drew in my head, and was turning around,
Down the chimney St Nicholas came with a bound.

He was dressed all in fur, from his head to his foot,
And his clothes were all tarnished with ashes and soot;
A bundle of toys he had flung on his back,
And he looked like a pedlar just opening his pack.
His eyes – how they twinkled! his dimples, how merry!
His cheeks were like roses, his nose like a cherry!

His droll little mouth was drawn up like a bow,
And the beard of his chin was as white as the snow;
He had a broad face and a little round belly
That shook, when he laughed, like a bowl full of jelly.

He was chubby and plump, a right jolly old elf,
And I laughed when I saw him, in spite of myself;
A wink of his eye and a twist of his head
Soon gave me to know I had nothing to dread;
He spoke not a word, but went straight to his work,
And filled all the stockings; then turned with a jerk,
And laying his fingers aside of his nose,
And giving a nod, up the chimney he rose;
He sprang to his sleigh, to his team gave a whistle,
And away they all flew like the down of a thistle.

But I heard him exclaim, ere he drove out of sight,
'Happy Christmas to all, and to all a good night!'

Clement Clarke Moore

While Shepherds Watched Their Flocks

While shepherds watched their flocks by night,
All seated on the ground,
The angel of the Lord came down,
And glory shone around.

'Fear not,' said he (for mighty dread
Had seized their troubled mind);
'Glad tidings of great joy I bring
To you and all mankind.

'To you in David's town this day
Is born of David's line
A Saviour, who is Christ the Lord;
And this shall be the sign:

44

'The heavenly Babe you there shall find
To human view displayed,
All meanly wrapped in swathing bands,
And in a manger laid.'

Thus spake the seraph; and forthwith
Appeared a shining throng
Of angels praising God, who thus
Addressed their joyful song:

'All glory be to God on high,
And to the earth be peace;
Goodwill henceforth from heaven to men
Begin and never cease.'

Nahum Tate

45

The Oxen

Christmas Eve, and twelve of the clock.
   'Now they are all on their knees,'
An elder said as we sat in a flock
   By the embers in hearthside ease.

We pictured the meek mild creatures where
   They dwelt in their strawy pen,
Nor did it occur to one of us there
   To doubt they were kneeling then.

So fair a fancy few would weave
   In these years! Yet, I feel,
If someone said on Christmas Eve,
   'Come; see the oxen kneel

'In the lonely barton by yonder coomb
   Our childhood used to know,'
I should go with him in the gloom,
   Hoping it might be so.

Thomas Hardy

Christmas Poem

Says a country legend told every year:
Go to the barn on Christmas Eve and see
what the creatures do as that long night tips over.
Down on their knees they will go, the fire
of an old memory whistling through their minds!

So I went. Wrapped to my eyes against the cold
I creaked back the barn door and peered in.
From town the church bells spilled their midnight
    music,
and the beasts listened –
yet they lay in their stalls like stone.

Oh the heretics!
Not to remember Bethlehem,
or the star as bright as a sun,
or the child born on a bed of straw!
To know only of the dissolving Now!

Still they drowsed on –
citizens of the pure, the physical world,
they loomed in the dark: powerful
of body, peaceful of mind,
innocent of history.

Brothers! I whispered. It is Christmas!
And you are no heretics, but a miracle,
immaculate still as when you thundered forth
on the morning of creation!
As for Bethlehem, that blazing star

still sailed the dark, but only looked for me.
Caught in its light, listening again to its story,
I curled against some sleepy beast, who nuzzled
my hair as though I were a child, and warmed me
the best it could all night.

Mary Oliver

Bells Ringing

I heard bells ringing
Suddenly all together, one wild, intricate figure,
A mixture of wonder and praise
Climbing the winter-winged air in December.
Norwich, Gloucester, Salisbury, combined with York
To shake Worcester and Paul's into the old discovery
Made frost-fresh again.
I heard these rocketing and wound-remembering chimes
Running their blessed counterpoint
Round the mazes of my mind,
And felt their message brimming over with love,
Watering my cold heart,
Until, as over all England hundreds of towers trembled
Beneath the force of Christmas rolling out,
I knew, as shepherds and magi knew,
That all sounds had been turned into one sound,
And a single golden bell,
Repeating, as knees bowed, the name EMMANUEL.

Leonard Clark

I Saw Three Ships

I saw three ships come sailing in,
Come sailing in, come sailing in;
I saw three ships come sailing in,
On Christmas Day in the morning.
And what was in those ships all three,
Those ships all three, those ships all three?
And what was in those ships all three,
On Christmas Day in the morning?
Our Saviour Christ and his lady,
And his lady, and his lady;
Our Saviour Christ and his lady,
On Christmas Day in the morning.

Anon.

Christmas Morning

Last year
on Christmas morning
we got up really early
and took the dog for a walk
across the downs.
It wasn't snowing
but the hills were white with frost
and our breath froze
in the air.
Judy rushed around like a crazy thing
as though Christmas
meant something special to her.
The sheep huddled together
looking tired
as if they'd been up all night
watching the stars.

We stood at the highest point
and thought about what Christmas means
and looked over the white hills
and looked up at the blue sky.
And the hills seemed
to go on forever
and the sky knew no bounds
and you could imagine
a world at peace.

Roger Stevens

Father Christmas sent me to the Moon

I don't know how he put it there:
our gas fire blocked the chimney
and the green rug where I played
had never magically flown for me.

But there it was – a telescope,
unwrapped but still a mystery,
centred like a compass needle
pointing the way to my heart.

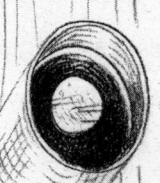

I lifted it to the window, lowered its legs
like a newborn lamb's and opened
its eye to a world still waiting
to be cratered by snowballs.

I took my first footsteps before I could breathe,
when I looked at the Moon and learned to believe.

Dom Conlon

Christmas Present

This year's ghosts of Christmases past
hang holly wreaths in the empty halls
they need no handle, lock or latch
spirits mulled in wine and warmth
somewhere the spark of kindness waits
beneath the carefully chosen gifts
on glittering glasses, gilded plates
fragrant ginger and cinnamon sticks
and I have wished for the stars above
a little snow and winter cheer
but just for now to hold the ones I love
and to know them safe as they are dear

Sue Hardy-Dawson

To Mrs K., On Her Sending Me an English Christmas Plum-Cake at Paris

What crowding thoughts around me wake,
What marvels in a Christmas-cake!
Ah say, what strange enchantment dwells
Enclosed within its odorous cells?
Is there no small magician bound
Encrusted in its snowy round?
For magic surely lurks in this,
A cake that tells of vanished bliss;
A cake that conjures up to view
The early scenes, when life was new;
When memory knew no sorrows past,
And hope believed in joys that last! —
Mysterious cake, whose folds contain
Life's calendar of bliss and pain;
That speaks of friends for ever fled,
And wakes the tears I love to shed.

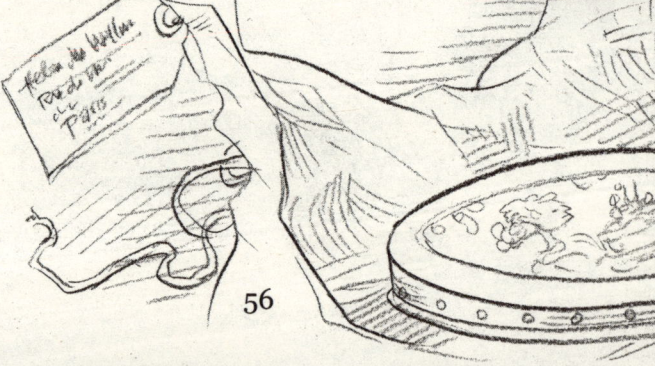

Oft shall I breathe her cherished name
From whose fair hand the offering came:
For she recalls the artless smile
Of nymphs that deck my native isle;
Of beauty that we love to trace,
Allied with tender, modest grace;
Of those who, while abroad they roam,
Retain each charm that gladdens home,
And whose dear friendships can impart
A Christmas banquet for the heart!

Helen Maria Williams

57

Talking Turkeys

Be nice to yu turkeys dis christmas
Cos' turkeys just wanna hav fun
Turkeys are cool, turkeys are wicked
An every turkey has a Mum.
Be nice to yu turkeys dis christmas,
Don't eat it, keep it alive,
It could be yu mate, an not on your plate
Say, Yo! Turkey I'm on your side.

I got lots of friends who are turkeys
An all of dem fear christmas time,
Dey wanna enjoy it, dey say humans destroyed it
An humans are out of dere mind,
Yeah, I got lots of friends who are turkeys
Dey all hav a right to a life,
Not to be caged up an genetically made up
By any farmer an his wife.

59

Turkeys just wanna play reggae
Turkeys just wanna hip-hop
Can yu imagine a nice young turkey saying,
'I cannot wait for de chop',
Turkeys like getting presents, dey wanna watch
   christmas TV,
Turkeys hav brains an turkeys feel pain
In many ways like yu an me.

I once knew a turkey called turkey
He said 'Benji explain to me please,
Who put de turkey in christmas
An what happens to christmas trees?',
I said 'I am not too sure turkey
But it's nothing to do wid Christ Mass
Humans get greedy an waste more dan need be
An business men mek loadsa cash'.

61

Be nice to yu turkey dis christmas
Invite dem indoors fe sum greens
Let dem eat cake an let dem partake
In a plate of organic grown beans,
Be nice to yu turkey dis christmas
An spare dem de cut of de knife,
Join Turkeys United an dey'll be delighted
An yu will mek new friends 'FOR LIFE'.

Benjamin Zephaniah

Hark

Drink up the mull till you're full
Don't mince on the pies
It's the season to gourmandize
Stock up on the stockings
Crack up with the crackers
The chimney looks the same
But Santa's gotten fatter
Time to be reckless
With the turkey in your trolley
Feel free to be legless
In front of the telly

Now with the innards fully filled
Spare a thought for tender words –
Peace. Share. Goodwill.

John Agard

The Twelve Days of Christmas

On the first day of Christmas
My true love sent to me
A partridge in a pear tree.

On the second day of Christmas
My true love sent to me
Two turtle doves,
And a partridge in a pear tree.

On the third day of Christmas
My true love sent to me
Three French hens, two turtle doves,
And a partridge in a pear tree.

On the fourth day of Christmas
My true love sent to me
Four calling birds, three French hens,
Two turtle doves, and a partridge in a pear tree.

On the fifth day of Christmas
My true love sent to me
Five gold rings, four calling birds,
Three French hens, two turtle doves,
And a partridge in a pear tree.

On the sixth day of Christmas
My true love sent to me
Six geese a-laying, five gold rings,
Four calling birds, three French hens,
Two turtle doves, and a partridge in a pear tree.

On the seventh day of Christmas
My true love sent to me
Seven swans a-swimming, six geese a-laying,
Five gold rings, four calling birds,
Three French hens, two turtle doves,
And a partridge in a pear tree.

On the eighth day of Christmas
My true love sent to me
Eight maids a-milking, seven swans a-swimming,
Six geese a-laying, five gold rings,
Four calling birds, three French hens,
Two turtle doves, and a partridge in a pear tree.

On the ninth day of Christmas
My true love sent to me
Nine drummers drumming, eight maids a-milking,
Seven swans a-swimming, six geese a-laying,
Five gold rings, four calling birds,
Three French hens, two turtle doves,
And a partridge in a pear tree.

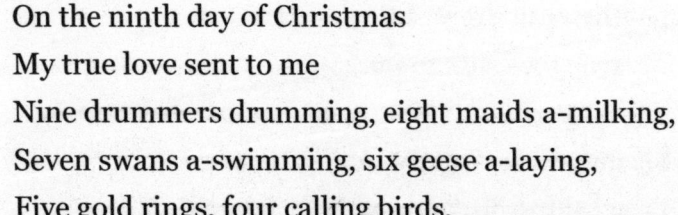

On the tenth day of Christmas
My true love sent to me
Ten pipers piping, nine drummers drumming,
Eight maids a-milking, seven swans a-swimming,
Six geese a-laying, five gold rings,
Four calling birds, three French hens,
Two turtle doves, and a partridge in a pear tree.

On the eleventh day of Christmas
My true love sent to me
Eleven ladies dancing, ten pipers piping,
Nine drummers drumming, eight maids a-milking,
Seven swans a-swimming, six geese a-laying,
Five gold rings, four calling birds,
Three French hens, two turtle doves,
And a partridge in a pear tree.

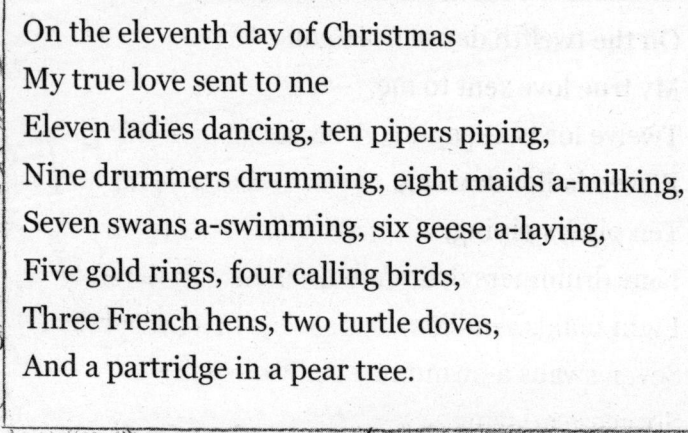

On the twelfth day of Christmas
My true love sent to me
Twelve lords a-leaping,
Eleven ladies dancing,
Ten pipers piping,
Nine drummers drumming,
Eight maids a-milking,
Seven swans a-swimming,
Six geese a-laying,
Five gold rings,
Four calling birds,
Three French hens,
Two turtle doves,
And a partridge in a pear tree.

Anon.

On the thirteenth day of Christmas my true love phoned me up...

Well, I suppose I should be grateful, you've obviously gone
to a lot of trouble and expense – or maybe off your head.
Yes, I did like the birds – the small ones anyway were fun
if rather messy, but now the hens have roosted on my bed
and the rest are nested on the wardrobe. It's hard to
    sleep
with all that cooing, let alone the cackling of the geese
whose eggs are everywhere, but mostly in a broken
    smelly heap
on the sofa. No, why should I mind? I can't get any peace
anywhere – the lounge is full of drummers thumping
    tom-toms
and sprawling lords crashed out from manic leaping.
    The kitchen
is crammed with cows and milkmaids and smells of a
    million stink-bombs
and enough sour milk to last a year. The pipers? I'd
    forgotten them –
they were no trouble, I paid them and they went. But I
    can't get rid
of these young ladies. They won't stop dancing
    or turn the music down

and they're always in the bathroom, squealing as they skid
across the flooded floor. No, I don't need a plumber round,
it's just the swans – where else can they swim? Poor things,
I think they're going mad, like me. When I went to wash
my
hands one ate the soap, another swallowed the gold rings.
And the pear tree died. Too dry. So thanks for nothing,
love. Goodbye.

Dave Calder

Nothingmas Day

No it wasn't.

It was Nothingmas Day and all the children in Notown
were not tingling with excitement as they lay unawake
in their heaps.

D
 o
  w
   n
    s
     t
      a
       i
        r

s their parents were busily not placing
the last crackermugs, glimmerslips and sweetlumps on
the Nothingmas Tree.

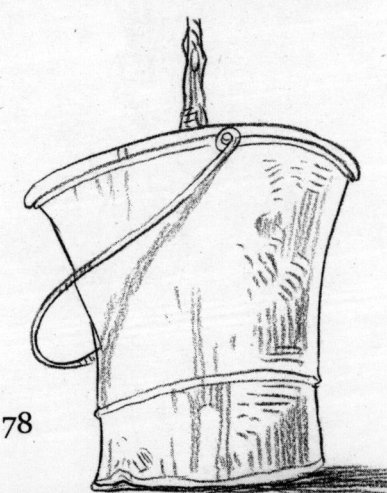

Hey! But what was that invisible trail of chummy sparks or vaulting stars across the sky?

Father Nothingmas – drawn by 18 or 21 rainmaidens!

Father Nothingmas – his sackbut bulging with air!

Father Nothingmas – was not on his way!

(From the streets of the snowless town came the quiet of unsung carols and the merry silence of the steeple bell.)

Next morning the children did not fountain out of bed with cries of WHOOPERATION! They picked up their Nothingmas Stockings and with traditional quiperamas such as: 'Look what I haven't got! It's just what I didn't want!' pulled their stockings on their ordinary legs.

For breakfast they ate – breakfast.

Afterwards they all avoided the Nothingmas Tree, where Daddy, his face failing to beam like a leaky torch, was not distributing gemgames, sodaguns, golly-trolleys, jars of humdrums and packets of slubberated croakers.

Off, off, off went the children to school, soaking each other with no howls of 'Merry Nothingmas and a Happy No Year!', and not pulping each other with no-balls.

At school Miss Whatnot taught them to write No Thank You Letters.

Home they burrowed for Nothingmas Dinner.
The table was not groaning under all manner of

No Turkey
No Spiced Ham
No Sprouts
No Cranberry Jellysauce
No Not Nowt

There was not one shoot of glee as the Nothingmas
Pudding, unlit, was not brought in. Mince pies were not
available, nor was there any demand for them.

Then, as another Nothingmas clobbered to a close, they all
haggled off to bed where they slept happily never after.

and that is not the end of the story . . .

Adrian Mitchell

Nicholas Was...

older than sin, and his beard could grow no whiter. He wanted to die.

The dwarfish natives of the Arctic caverns did not speak his language, but conversed in their own, twittering tongue, conducted incomprehensible rituals, when they were not actually working in the factories.

Once every year they forced him, sobbing and protesting, into Endless Night. During the journey he would stand near every child in the world, leave one of the dwarves' invisible gifts by its bedside. The children slept, frozen into time.

He envied Prometheus and Loki, Sisyphus and Judas.
His punishment was harsher.

Ho.

Ho.

Ho.

Neil Gaiman

Christmas Carol

The kings they came from out the south,
  All dressed in ermine fine;
They bore Him gold and chrysoprase,
  And gifts of precious wine.

The shepherds came from out the north,
  Their coats were brown and old;
They brought Him little new-born lambs –
  They had not any gold.

The wise men came from out the east,
  And they were wrapped in white;
The star that led them all the way
  Did glorify the night.

The angels came from heaven high,
  And they were clad with wings;
And lo, they brought a joyful song
  The host of heaven sings.

The kings they knocked upon the door,
  The wise men entered in,
The shepherds followed after them
  To hear the song begin.

The angels sang through all the night
  Until the rising sun,
But little Jesus fell asleep
  Before the song was done.

Sara Teasdale

We Three Kings

We three kings of Orient are;
Bearing gifts we traverse afar
Field and fountain, moor and mountain,
Following yonder star.

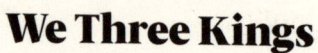

O star of wonder, star of night,
Star with royal beauty bright,
Westward leading, still proceeding,
Guide us to thy perfect light.

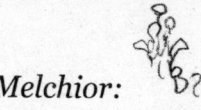

Melchior:

Born a king on Bethlehem's plain,
Gold I bring, to crown Him again –
King for ever, ceasing never,
Over us all to reign.

Gaspar: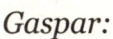

Frankincense to offer have I;
Incense owns a Deity nigh:
Prayer and praising, voices raising,
Worship him, God most high.

Balthazar:

Myrrh is mine; its bitter perfume
Breathes a life of gathering gloom;
Sorrowing, sighing, bleeding, dying,
Sealed in the stone-cold tomb.

All:

Glorious now, behold Him arise,
King, and God, and sacrifice!
Heaven sings alleluia,
Alleluia the earth replies!

O star of wonder, star of night,
Star with royal beauty bright,
Westward leading, still proceeding,
Guide us to thy perfect light.

John Henry Hopkins

A Christmas Poem

When my Great -Aunt Bertha,
who was a Quaker,
read in the papers
of how their boys and our boys gave it all up,
put the guns down
and climbed over the top
to kick the patched leather ball
between barbed wire and crater rims,
between the two straight dark ditches they lived in,
she took it upon herself to head down to Woolworth's
and buy up all the marked down boxes of Christmas cards,
lolling on the January shelves.

She spent her war years licking stamps,

inking addresses,

printing xmas messages in one of a number of different
languages,

as appropriate,

signing her love

and visiting the pillar-box at the head of her road.

Sacks of the things went off at once,

whole stretches of trench filled with spade-handled robins,

holly, magi, stockings and snow.

The babe of peace arrived in his manger,
in the stable,
in March, in April, in May,
ceaselessly,
year on year.

If there had been no calendars,
no officers, no orders,
no today's or yesterday's newspaper in the mess,
in the trench,
no date on the soldier's letter from home,
then her plan may have worked,
assuming the other side were equally ill-equipped
and open-mindedly eager to clutch peace as it passed.

But
no one was stupid enough to think it might be Christmas
every day,
no one was fooled by her hand,
and besides, the ball
needed pumping
and a puncture repair kit.
Great-Aunt Bertha.

A. F. Harrold

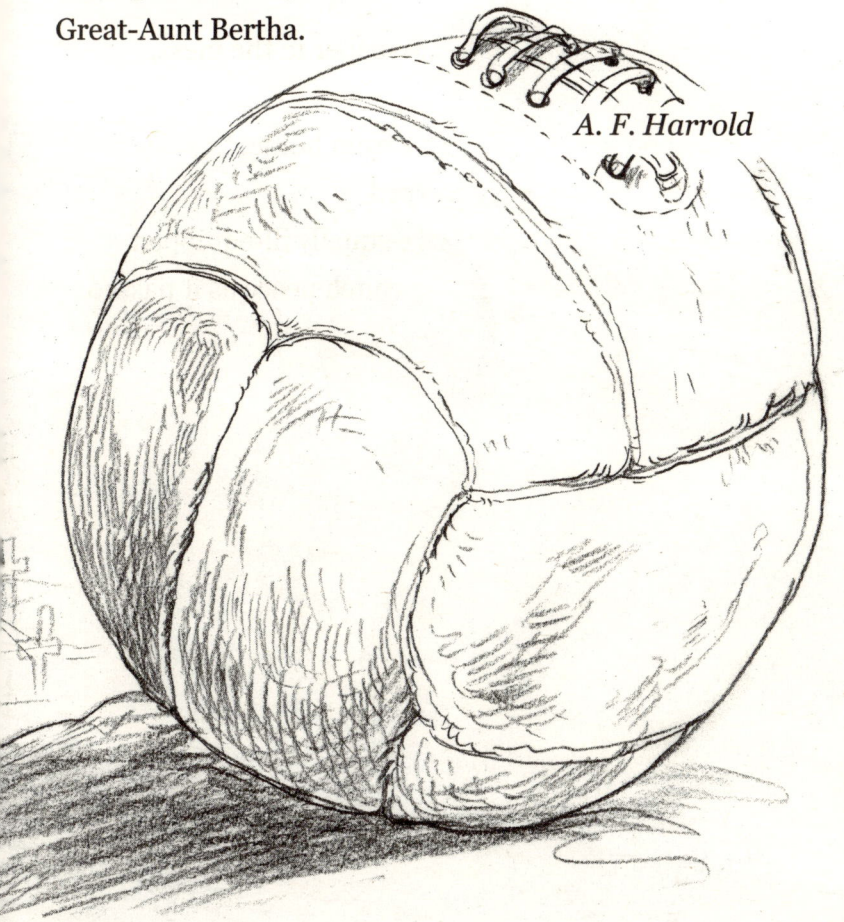

Let There Be Peace

Let there be peace
So frowns fly away like albatross
And skeletons foxtrot from cupboards;
So war correspondents become travel show presenters
And magpies bring back lost property,
Children, engagement rings, broken things.

Let there be peace
So storms can go out to sea to be
Angry and return to me calm,
So the broken can rise and dance in the hospitals.
Let the aged Ethiopian man in the grey block of flats
Peer through his window and see Addis before him
So his thrilled outstretched arms become frames
For his dreams.

Let there be peace
Let tears evaporate to form clouds, cleanse themselves
And fall into reservoirs of drinking water.
Let harsh memories burst into fireworks that melt
In the dark pupils of a child's eyes
And disappear like shoals of darting silver fish.
And let the waves reach the shore with a

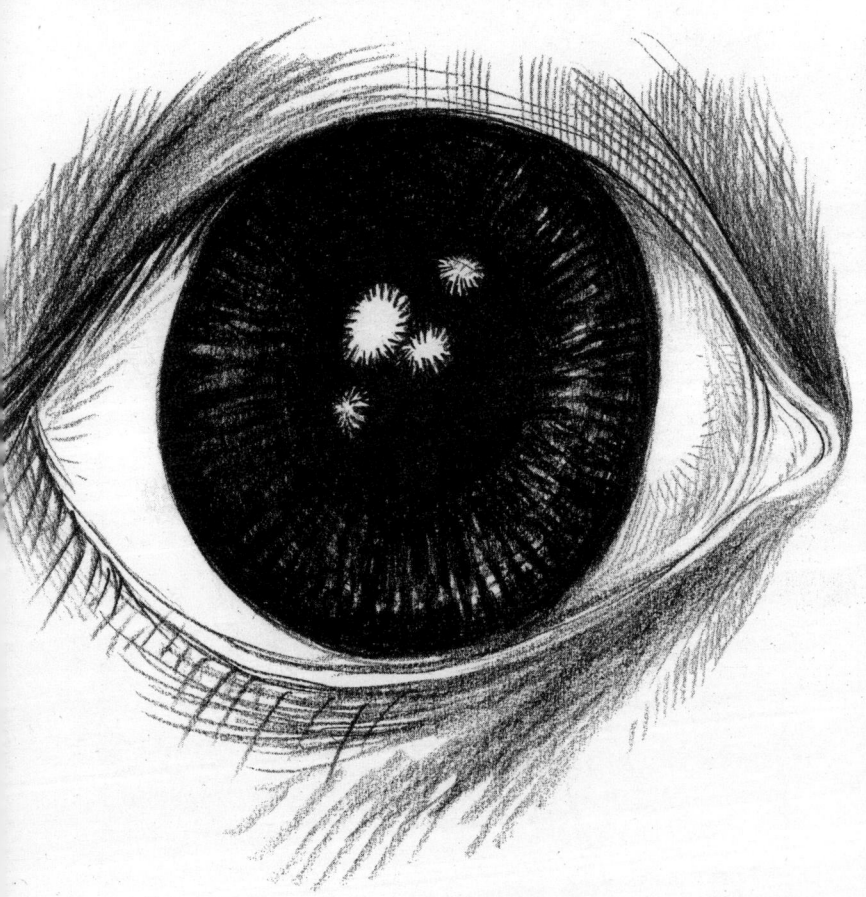

Shhhhhhhhh Shhhhhhhh Shhhhhhhhhh.

Lemn Sissay

Ring Out, Wild Bells (*from* In Memoriam)

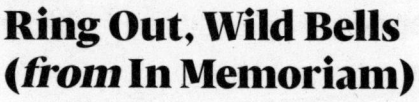

Ring out, wild bells, to the wild sky,
    The flying cloud, the frosty light:
    The year is dying in the night;
Ring out, wild bells, and let him die.

Ring out the old, ring in the new,
    Ring, happy bells, across the snow:
    The year is going, let him go;
Ring out the false, ring in the true.

Ring out the grief that saps the mind
  For those that here we see no more;
  Ring out the feud of rich and poor,
Ring in redress to all mankind.

Ring out a slowly dying cause,
  And ancient forms of party strife;
  Ring in the nobler modes of life,
With sweeter manners, purer laws.

Ring out the want, the care, the sin,
   The faithless coldness of the times;
   Ring out, ring out my mournful rhymes
But ring the fuller minstrel in.

Ring out false pride in place and blood,
   The civic slander and the spite;
   Ring in the love of truth and right,
Ring in the common love of good.

Ring out old shapes of foul disease;
    Ring out the narrowing lust of gold;
    Ring out the thousand wars of old,
Ring in the thousand years of peace.

Ring in the valiant man and free,
    The larger heart, the kindlier hand;
    Ring out the darkness of the land,
Ring in the Christ that is to be.

Alfred, Lord Tennyson

Balloons

Since Christmas they have lived with us,
Guileless and clear,
Oval soul-animals,
Taking up half the space,
Moving and rubbing on the silk

Invisible air drifts,
Giving a shriek and pop
When attacked, then scooting to rest, barely trembling.
Yellow cathead, blue fish——
Such queer moons we live with

Instead of dead furniture!
Straw mats, white walls
And these travelling
Globes of thin air, red, green,
Delighting

The heart like wishes or free
Peacocks blessing
Old ground with a feather
Beaten in starry metals.
Your small

Brother is making
His balloon squeak like a cat.
Seeming to see
A funny pink world he might eat on the other side of it,
He bites,

Then sits
Back, fat jug
Contemplating a world clear as water.
A red
Shred in his little fist.

Sylvia Plath

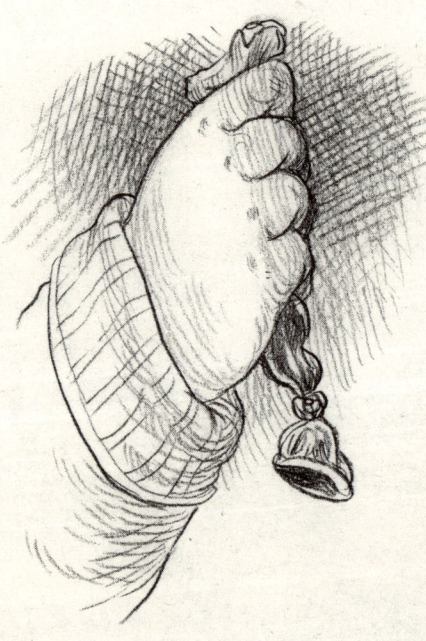

Good Riddance, But Now What?

Come, children, gather round my knee;
Something is about to be.

Tonight's December thirty-first,
Something is about to burst.

The clock is crouching, dark and small,
Like a time bomb in the hall.

Hark! It's midnight, children dear.
Duck! Here comes another year.

Ogden Nash

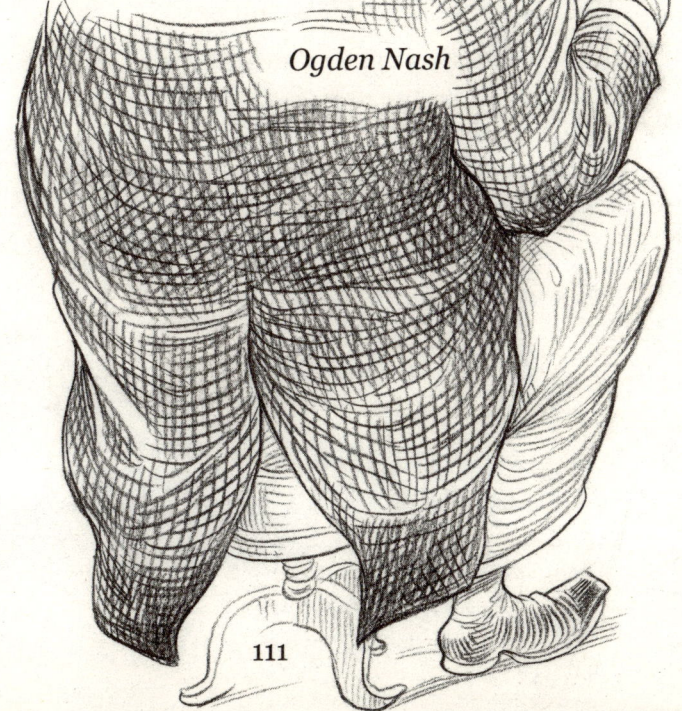

Auld Lang Syne

Should auld acquaintance be forgot
>And never brought to mind?
Should auld acquaintance be forgot,
>And auld lang syne?

For auld lang syne, my dear,
>*For auld lang syne.*
We'll tak a cup o' kindness yet,
>*For auld lang syne.*

And surely ye'll be your pint stoup,
>And surely I'll be mine;
And we'll tak a cup o' kindness yet,
>For auld lang syne.

We twa hae run about the braes,
>And pou'd the gowans fine;
But we've wander'd mony a weary fit,
>Sin' auld lang syne.

We twa hae paidl'd in the burn,
Frae morning sun till dine;
But seas between us braid hae roar'd
Sin' auld lang syne.

And there's a hand, my trusty fiere!
And gie's a hand o' thine!
And we'll tak a right gude-willie waught,
For auld lang syne.

Robert Burns

Promise

Remember, the time of year
when the future appears
like a blank sheet of paper
a clean calendar, a new chance.
On thick white snow

you vow fresh footprints
then watch them go
with the wind's hearty gust.
Fill your glass. Here's tae us. Promises
made to be broken, made to last.

Jackie Kay

Index of First Lines

Index of Poets

Acknowledgements

The compiler and publisher would like to thank the following for permission to use their copyright material:

Agard, John, Hark copyright © John Agard 2010 reproduced by kind permission of John Agard c/o Caroline Sheldon Literary Agency Ltd. Green Magi copyright © John Agard 2010 reproduced by kind permission of John Agard c/o Caroline Sheldon Literary Agency Ltd.**Bevan, Clare,** 'Just Doing My Job' First published by: Macmillan. Edited by Brain Moses, 1998. **Bloom, Valerie,** Christmas Is Here © Valerie Bloom 2000 from Let Me Touch the Sky (Macmillan) reprinted by permission of Eddison Pearson Ltd on behalf of Valerie Bloom. **Calder, Dave,** 'We are Not Alone' and 'On the Thirteenth Day of Christmas My True Love Phoned Me Up...' reprinted by permission of the poet. **Clark, Leonard,** 'Bells Ringing', by permission of Robert Clark, Literary Executor of the author. **Conlon, Dom,** 'Father Christmas Sent Me to the Moon' First published in This Rock That Rock, Troika Books 2020. **Cope, Wendy,** 'The Christmas Life' from If I Don't Know (Faber and Faber), reprinted by permission of Faber and Faber Ltd. **Dean, Jan,** 'Angels' reprinted by permission of the poet. **Dhaker, Imtiaz,** 'Mumbai Kissmiss' Over the Moon (Bloodaxe Books, 2014) Reproduced with permission of Bloodaxe Books. **Gaiman, Neil,** Nicholas Was copyright © 1989 by Neil Gaiman. Reprinted by permission of Writers House LLC acting as agent for the author. **Hardy-Dawson, Sue,** 'Christmas Present' reprinted by permission of the poet. **Harrold, A.F.,** 'A CHRISTMAS POEM' from THINGS YOU FIND IN A POETS' BEARD (BURNING EYE BOOKS, 2015). © A.F. Harold. Reproduced by kind permission of the poet. **Haselhurst, Maureen,** 'Christmas at Four Winds Farm' reprinted by permission of the poet. **Kay, Jackie,** 'Promises' Darling: New & Selected Poems (Bloodaxe Books, 2007) by permission of the publisher. **McGough, Roger,** 'The Snowman' from 100 Best Christmas